HISTORY DUDES
VIKINGS

WRITTEN BY
LAURA BULLER

ILLUSTRATED BY
RICH CANDO

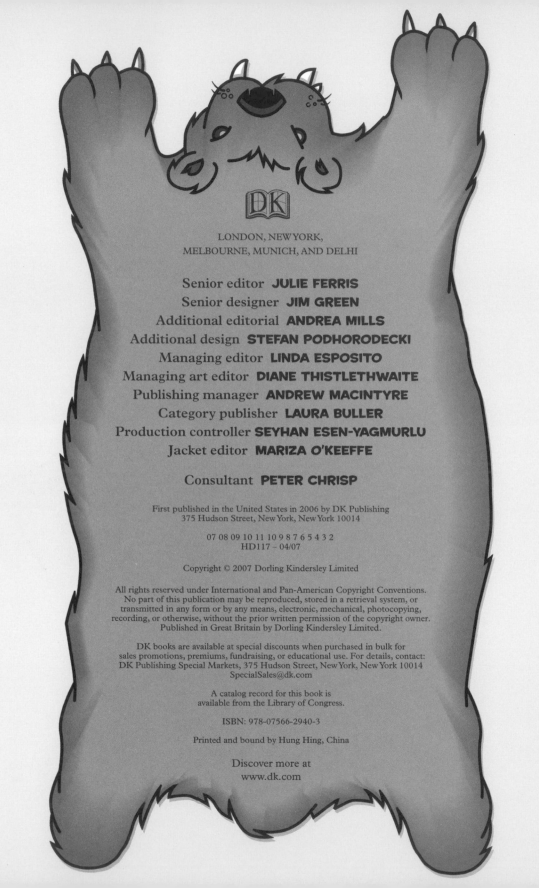

DK

LONDON, NEW YORK,
MELBOURNE, MUNICH, AND DELHI

Senior editor **JULIE FERRIS**
Senior designer **JIM GREEN**
Additional editorial **ANDREA MILLS**
Additional design **STEFAN PODHORODECKI**
Managing editor **LINDA ESPOSITO**
Managing art editor **DIANE THISTLETHWAITE**
Publishing manager **ANDREW MACINTYRE**
Category publisher **LAURA BULLER**
Production controller **SEYHAN ESEN-YAGMURLU**
Jacket editor **MARIZA O'KEEFFE**

Consultant **PETER CHRISP**

First published in the United States in 2006 by DK Publishing
375 Hudson Street, New York, New York 10014

07 08 09 10 11 10 9 8 7 6 5 4 3 2
HD117 – 04/07

DK books are available at special discounts when purchased in bulk for
sales promotions, premiums, fundraising, or educational use. For details, contact:
DK Publishing Special Markets, 375 Hudson Street, New York, New York 10014
SpecialSales@dk.com

A catalog record for this book is
available from the Library of Congress.

ISBN: 978-07566-2940-3

Printed and bound by Hung Hing, China

Discover more at
www.dk.com

CONTENTS

Hurry up and turn the page— I'm late for a raid.

Vikings ahoy!

It's early June in 793, and monks on the English isle of Lindisfarne spot ships on the horizon. They're curious—has someone ordered a pizza? But as the ships get closer, their curiosity turns to terror. On board are lots of dodgy-looking dudes, waving swords, axes, and spears. They pile off and wade ashore. From their battle cries, they're ready for a big-time rumble. These men are not delivering a take-out, they are bringing mayhem. The dudes of Lindisfarne and the monastery treasures are in grave danger. The Vikings have landed.

The monks of Lindisfarne are shaking in their sandals. They are completely at the mercy of these scary invaders. Some monks are captured for a life of slavery, while others are sent to their maker. Soon, there is no one left to protect the monastery treasures: beautiful manuscripts decorated with gems, glorious wall tapestries, ivory chests, silver bowls, and golden statues. The Vikings bag up all the good stuff and load it on their ships. They even rip the jeweled covers from the Bibles and shred the insides. Anything they don't take, they destroy. The church and outbuildings are set alight and the raiders head home with the stolen goods and stolen dudes.

But who are the Vikings, and where do they come from? More importantly, what do they have against shaving? Well, here goes. These hairy dudes hail from the northern European lands of Norway, Denmark, and Sweden. Many are farmers and craftspeople, but they're also super sailors and shipbuilders. With these skills, they can explore and trade far away from their homelands.

Maybe the raid at Lindisfarne hasn't given you a very good first impression of the Vikings. It's true, these dudes don't always play nice. It's also true that they are renowned for violent sea raids on wealthy targets. But not all Vikings are nasty pieces of work—honest. Come and meet some. Just sit back, relax, and turn the page, dude...

Viking Longship

With its fearsome figurehead and billowing, blood-red sail, the Viking longship is one radical ride. Sleek and speedy, the drekar, or dragon-headed longship, is sturdy enough to withstand stormy seas, yet light enough to travel up inland rivers. Viking warriors can cross the oceans under sail then switch to oar power for sneak attacks. Its low, broad shape means a ship can sail in the shallows and land right on the beach to spill out a load of raiders, ready to bring mayhem.

Weathervane (shows wind direction)

Mast (pole to hold sail and rigging)

1 Tip to tail, the average longship is 98 ft (30 m) long and carries 60 men and their gear.

2 Near the stern, a helmsman steers the ship with a large steering oar, lashed to the ship with leather cord.

3 The stern is thin and curved, so the boat can go backward without having to turn around—very handy for making a quick escape.

4 Storytelling—especially tales of the mighty Viking gods—provides on-board entertainment for the crew.

Stern (back of ship)

5 Long, thick planks of wood (usually oak) are fastened with iron nails to a sturdy keel, and then to each other, one plank overlapping the next.

6 Spaces between the wooden planks are filled with animal fur or moss drenched in tar, to make the ship watertight.

Dolphin (quite smart)

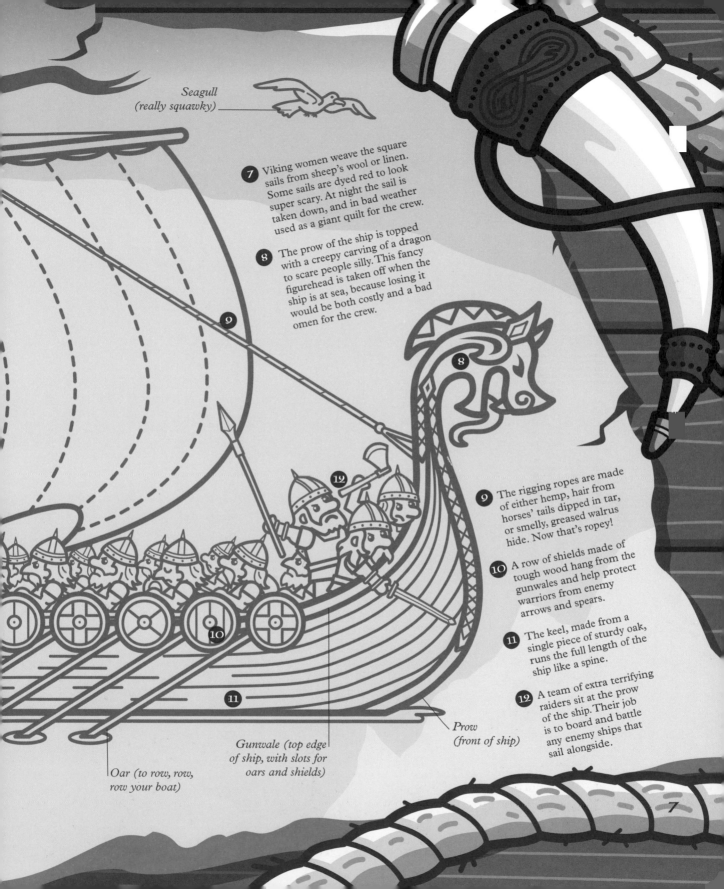

Seagull (really squawky)

7 Viking women weave the square sails from sheep's wool or linen. Some sails are dyed red to look super scary. At night the sail is taken down, and in bad weather used as a giant quilt for the crew.

8 The prow of the ship is topped with a creepy carving of a dragon to scare people silly. This fancy figurehead is taken off when the ship is at sea, because losing it would be both costly and a bad omen for the crew.

8

9 The rigging ropes are made of either hemp, hair from horses' tails dipped in tar, or smelly, greased walrus hide. Now that's ropey!

10 A row of shields made of tough wood hang from the gunwales and help protect warriors from enemy arrows and spears.

11 The keel, made from a single piece of sturdy oak, runs the full length of the ship like a spine.

12 A team of extra terrifying raiders sit at the prow of the ship. Their job is to board and battle any enemy ships that sail alongside.

Prow (front of ship)

Gunwale (top edge of ship, with slots for oars and shields)

Oar (to row, row, row your boat)

Bjorn the Berserk

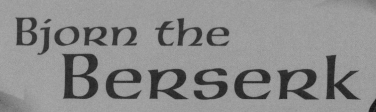

Mean and mad, berserkers work themselves up into a terrifying rage before a battle. Let's catch up with one of these famously fearsome dudes in one of his quieter moments. Hopefully...

It's a shaggy bear story...

Q: *So you're a berserker. Cool name. What does it mean, exactly?*

A: Even I don't remember why we're called berserkers. A *sekr* is our word for a shirt, and some dudes think berserk means "bear shirt." Some of us do go into battle wearing big hairy bearskins, like shirts. But others don't wear anything at all. Those nude dudes say berserk means "bare of shirt."

Q: *Dude, what's with the bearskins anyway? Are you trying to scare people or something?*

A: That's the idea. When we wear the bearskin, we become possessed by the living animal's spirit. Some of us even believe that we can morph into bears as we fight, and take on the animal's form and shape. Grrr.

Q: *Please stop, you're making me nervous. Say it's the day of a big battle. Can you tell us what's on your to-do list?*

A: The key is to get the rage thing going. It can take hours. I might paint my face and wear the bearskin because it's all about looking really scary. Then I add the sound effects—howling...snorting...growling—sometimes I scare myself. To really get into it I bang a couple of helmets together or try to bite a chunk from my shield. Sometimes my face swells up and turns purple. Before long I'm a full-on, foaming-at-the-mouth berserker, ready to rip. When the rage takes hold, I feel invincible—nothing can stop me and no weapons can harm me.

Q: *Talk us through a typical tussle. Do you use any special tactics on the battlefield?*

A: Sometimes there are a dozen of us fighting together, other times we stand alone. There are no rules. We just give it everything we've got and let the rage take over. If we're outnumbered, we form a tight circle and lash out at our attackers from there.

Whoooo's got a screw loose?

Bit of warpaint...

...test the old gnashers...

...and kaboom!

Q: *Some reports have you attacking trees, rocks—even your own people. Dude, what's up with that?*

A: What can I say? The rage makes it hard to think straight. We'll attack anything, anyone, anywhere, and if that includes the odd boulder or two, so be it. Nothing can stand in our way.

Q: *That is pretty intense, dude. Where do you think all that rage comes from? What makes you behave like that?*

A: Well, there are rumors that some of us have a few strong drinks or a few magical mushrooms before the rage takes hold. But I'm not telling.

Q: *You're pretty tight with Odin, the god of war. Can you tell us about your special relationship?*

A: Odin is everything, dude. He protects us better than any shield could, and he's the one who gives us our superhuman strength on the battlefield. If things don't work out and we die a heroic death, the dude has booked a place for us in Valhalla, his fancy pad in the afterlife. Sometimes they call us the "Odin Men" because we are so loyal.

Q: *Surely there must be down time. What do you do when you aren't fighting?*

A: We've got work to do like everyone else. Say we've got a tough job that needs a lot of muscle, we just turn on that berserk rage to help us. We do a little shivering, our teeth chatter, then we blow hot and cold, kind of like a fever. When the rage finally takes over we're strong enough to get the job done. Got to tell you, though, it really takes it out of you. When we crash, we're weaker than kittens.

Q: *One last thing… have you considered faux fur?*

A: Grrrrr.

Let's get ready to rumble...

Take that, you hunk of trunk!

Meow... I mean, grrrrRRRRRowl!

9

Weapons of war

*Ask a Viking warrior to name the thing he treasures most.
Chances are it won't be his mom, but another battleaxe (or
sword, spear, or shield). Viking raiders even give their weapons
nicknames, like Leg Biter, Peace Breaker, or Old Faithful.
In death, a Viking's favorite weapon gets buried
alongside him. Battle on, dude.*

Cutting edge

Viking swords are hammered into shape
from iron, with a sharp point for thrusting
and a sturdy hilt (handle) for a good grip.
Most swords are double-edged, so both sides
of the blade can cut and slice. It's important
because Vikings hold a sword with only one
hand—the other holds a shield.

Common chopper

The most widely owned Viking weapon, a battleaxe,
is about an arm's length long, with a brutal blade
attached to a long handle. While swords are good
for slashing, an axe blade is more effective for heavy,
smashing blows. It can even slice off the top of a
dude's head. The sturdy wooden handle means an
axe is less likely to break than a sword.

Dude defence

Round and made of wood, a sturdy shield blocks incoming blows
from swords or arrows. An iron bump called a boss helps protect the
warrior's hand. He holds his shield steady with a leather handle on the
other side of the boss. Some people paint their shields or decorate them
with drawings of the gods.

Breezy banner

Brave warriors raise their weapons in battle, but they also need to lift their spirits. This raven banner, which is sacred to Odin, the god of war, does the trick. When the banner catches the wind, the raven seems to fly. This inspires dudes to do their best, by doing their worst to the enemy.

Look sharp!

One look at a Viking spear and you get the point. Bigger, heavier spears are used when up close and personal with an opponent. One powerful thrust can skewer a dude like a kebab. Lightweight spears with razor-sharp tips are thrown from a distance to rain down on the enemy.

C'mon, let's rumble. Are you a man or a mouse?

Headfirst

To keep the old noggin in good nick, warriors wear helmets. The most common style is a close-fitting bowl shape made of leather or iron. Fancier helmets have goggles to protect the eyes, or a nose guard—a strip of metal down the center to shield the schnozz.

Get lost, cat bait, before I start splitting hairs.

Shielding an attack

Someone's got an axe to grind? Don't hide behind your shield, dude. Use it as a weapon. Get right in your opponent's face, the closer the better.

Now push his shield up into his face with yours. He should drop the axe faster than a hot potato, while leaving his backside exposed for a swift sword attack.

Fighting talk

Oh dear, here comes a spear. When facing such a pointed attack, defend yourself, dude. Pull your sword and shield close to your body right away.

As the spear thrusts, swing your shield away from your body to deflect the blow. Then simply lop off the spear tip and go in for the kill.

Homestead

There's plenty of hustle and bustle on a typical Viking homestead—and always something that needs doing. Thankfully there are a lot of helping hands, as the whole extended family lives and works on the farm. These dudes pretty much grow, make, raise, or build everything they need, from the clothes on their backs to the dinner on the table. So, let's go down on the farm where it's all happening.

A shore bet

Life's a beach for the Vikings who build their homesteads on a fjord (sea inlet). Longboats loaded with goods or smaller passenger craft can rock right up to the dock and unload their cargo. Another hot spot for homes is on a hilltop. The awesome view of the surrounding area helps people spot arriving friends—or foes—quickly.

Gone fishing

Hungry Vikings who wish for fish can sink a hook and a line into the fjord and snag their supper. Some fish is gobbled up fresh, but most of the catch of the day is preserved and stored for winter. People sail farther afield (or even afjord) to hunt whales, seals, and walruses.

Stable mates

The animals hang out in their own houses. Hard-working horses that spend the days pulling wooden plows get to share the stables with cows, sheep, pigs, and goats. If it's really cold, cows sleep inside the longhouse with the family. The stink can be udderly awful.

Forest fodder

To you, it's pretty scenery. To the Vikings, it's like a department store. Trees make timber and fuel the fires, fjords are for fishing, and the wild animals roaming around, such as deer, moose, bears, and boars, are fair game for hunters.

Hey look! Here's lunch!

Full house

The whole clan—children, parents, grandparents, farm workers, and maybe a dog or two—live together as one big happy, smelly family in the longhouse. A typical house is 100 ft (30 m) in length and built with wood, stones, or earth. Outside the longhouse is a vegetable patch and fields of flax, wheat, or barley.

To the outhouse

When nature calls, Vikings answer in the latrine. Inside this simple wooden shelter, there's a deep and deeply stinky hole dug into the ground. Everything that comes out of a Viking goes right down into the hole, making a smelly soup that ensures no one lingers long.

Fish in the freeze

When the fjord freezes, Viking cooks can dish up a tasty air-dried fish. With the guts removed, fresh fish are hung up to dry in the cold air. Three months later, when the water in the fish has evaporated, they are stored. The rock-hard fish can break teeth, so must be soaked in water before eating.

Scram, beak face!

Heavy metal

Vikings have to make all the tools they need to work the farm, and fix them when they break. The man in charge of ironwork is the blacksmith. He's always banging on something, shaping iron in a super-hot forge, then bashing it around on a heavy iron block called an anvil.

Mealtime

You can't conquer new lands or work the one you own on an empty stomach. The Vikings enjoy a variety of tasty food and drinks. In a typical longhouse, there's plenty of buzz and bustle around the cooking fire. Let's meet the dudette in the middle of it all, and find out what's on the menu.

Q: *Excuse me, you look very busy, but could you please talk us through a typical day?*

A: Every day is different but one thing is the same—work, work, and more work. The chores begin at dawn. The first task is starting the fire—it's nippy in the mornings and we need the firelight, too. Next we feed the animals, milk the cows, and tend

to the crops. After all that, we're more than ready for dagmal, the first meal of the day.

Q: *Sounds mouthwatering. What do you eat?*

A: There's usually a bubbling cauldron (pot) of oat or wheat porridge on the go. It's a staple for farming families like mine—porridge sticks to the ribs. I serve it with a little bread and blubber.

Q: *Surely you mean butter?*

A: My name isn't Shirley. It's Ingrid. Yes, we do eat butter or we use seal blubber instead. It's delicious. Anyway, we wash our dagmal down with water or buttermilk served in drinking horns. Mine are animal horns, but fancier folks have silver horns.

Q: *After dagmal are you crazy busy or what?*

A: You're not kidding. Preparing food takes ages. The weather is harsh and fresh food isn't easy to get, so we find ways to make our edibles last.

Honey, I'm home!

So this is what they mean by the daily grind.

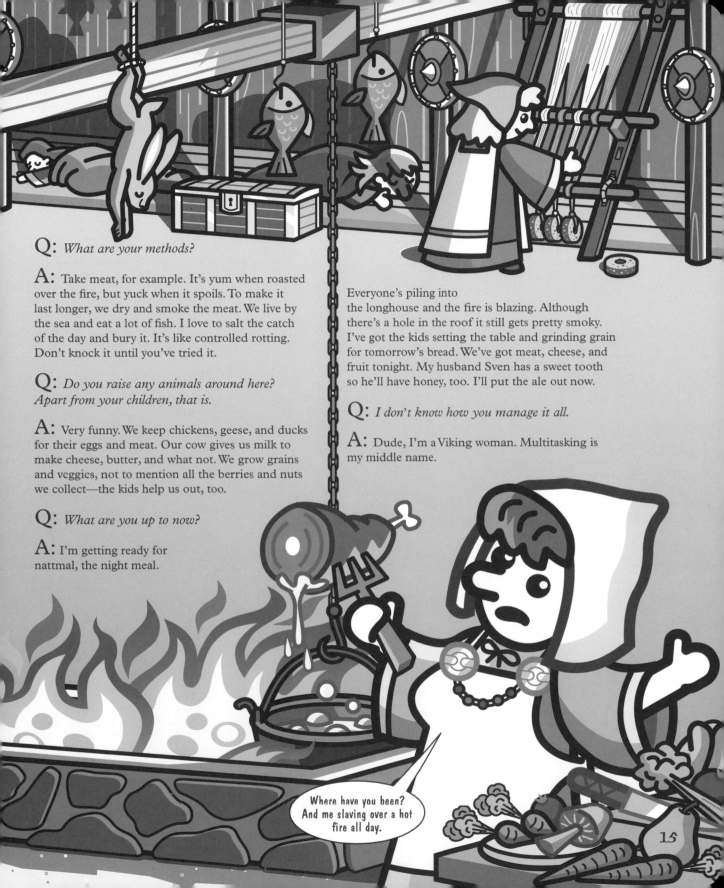

Q: *What are your methods?*

A: Take meat, for example. It's yum when roasted over the fire, but yuck when it spoils. To make it last longer, we dry and smoke the meat. We live by the sea and eat a lot of fish. I love to salt the catch of the day and bury it. It's like controlled rotting. Don't knock it until you've tried it.

Q: *Do you raise any animals around here? Apart from your children, that is.*

A: Very funny. We keep chickens, geese, and ducks for their eggs and meat. Our cow gives us milk to make cheese, butter, and what not. We grow grains and veggies, not to mention all the berries and nuts we collect—the kids help us out, too.

Q: *What are you up to now?*

A: I'm getting ready for nattmal, the night meal.

Everyone's piling into the longhouse and the fire is blazing. Although there's a hole in the roof it still gets pretty smoky. I've got the kids setting the table and grinding grain for tomorrow's bread. We've got meat, cheese, and fruit tonight. My husband Sven has a sweet tooth so he'll have honey, too. I'll put the ale out now.

Q: *I don't know how you manage it all.*

A: Dude, I'm a Viking woman. Multitasking is my middle name.

Where have you been? And me slaving over a hot fire all day.

15

Job opportunities

There's work aplenty for Vikings. Finding work is not the problem. The problem is finding time to do all the work that needs to be done. Luckily, Vikings have no problem with child labor. Young dudes must learn the skills needed to get the crops growing and the cows mooing. While dudettes get busy learning to cook, spin wool, and weave, their brothers often take up a craft or trade, such as shipbuilding or ironworking. By the time most Vikings hit their middle teens, they are married and working full time. Here's just some of the must-do jobs for Viking dudes.

Crazy dudes wanted

Are you willing to fight with reckless abandon? Berserkers needed to join summer invasion of neighboring land.

Raiders required

Join loads of like-minded Vikings, sail to new and exotic places, pillage treasures, and kill people. Armor and weapons not included.

Apprentice comb maker needed

Care about hair? Help your fellow dudes with their grooming by making combs from deer and elk antlers. In this skilled position you will learn how to create the handle from a pair of antlers by attaching them with iron rivets to either side of a thin rectangle of sliced antler. The tricky bit is cutting the comb teeth into the rectangle, but full training is provided. Contact Anskar, the master comb maker, at his workshop for further details.

Carpentry course

Woodworking is an incredibly important job and skilled carpenters are always in demand, whether they are knocking up a house from felled trees, crafting furniture, or creating a splendid sailing ship. Learn all the tricks of the trade and boost your earning potential by enrolling in Cnut's Carpentry College. The first 15 applicants will receive a bonus class on how to avoid splinters.

I couldn't do that. I'm as thick as two short planks.

Sweaty collar vacancy

Repairing, shaping, and working iron over a blazing fire—now that's a hot job. Bjorn the blacksmith is looking for an experienced metalworker to join his team. The successful dude will be crafting and creating everything from a raider's sword to a cook's cauldron and a chieftain's jewelry.

A belting opportunity

Tough dude needed for busy leatherworkers. Lars's Leathers produces some of the finest belts, shoes, boots, shield handles, carrying bags, storage pouches, and battlefield helmets in the whole of Denmark. Vacancy would suit a retired raider with the brute strength required to turn the animal skins into leather and to cut and stitch it. Immediate start.

Dress to impress

Never get into a spin making cloth again. Sign up for Sigga's Sewing School and learn how to turn a tuft of wool into string by spinning it on a wooden spindle.

Pay attention as Sigga teaches you how to change the color of the wool using homemade vegetable dyes.

She'll show you how to weave the wool into cloth on a loom—a frame, which holds up-and-down threads while you add rows of back-and-forth threads. Nimble fingers only please.

Helping hands wanted

The womenfolk of Birka require farmhands to help them tend the animals and harvest crops. The dudes of the village are away raiding, and the dudettes have too much to do already with all their household tasks. Applications from young, handsome dudes are especially welcome.

We could do a job share.

It would never work. Just like you.

17

Dude fashion

Hairstyles

Most Viking dudes have shoulder-length hair, although slaves wear their hair short. A comb-through keeps hairdos tidy and lifts out any nasty vermin.

Facial hair

Many men grow beards and mustaches. But warriors often don't. They don't want their enemies grabbing the growth!

Pants

Baggy or tight, depending on local style, pants are woven from wool or linen dyed in bright colors.

Leather shoes lined with fur keep tootsies toasty.

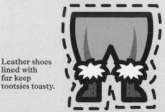

Caps are made of fox, deer, or bear fur.

Helmets include goggles to protect the eyes.

Headwear

A furry cap keeps the head warm and dry. On the battlefield, some Vikings opt for an iron helmet with chain mail attached to protect the neck.

Spearheads are stopped by the protective mesh.

Chain mail

These tough t-shirts are made of thousands of tiny iron rings linked together.

Viking men dress differently, depending on where they live, what they do, and how rich they are. Most dudes wear a basic wardrobe of woven pants, leather shoes, an undertunic, and a protective overtunic. A leather belt holds everything up, a cloak and cap keep out wintry winds, and jewelry adds dazzle.

Awesome arm ring

Necklace with cool pendant

Jewelry

Vikings love bling! Silver, bronze, gold, and bone...pile it on, dude! The brighter, the better.

A brooch can pull a look together.

Personal hygiene

Wash time

An Arab dude says he saw a Viking slave bringing a basin of water to the man of the house, who washed his hands and face, then blew his nose and spat into the water. The next family member had a turn, and so on. We can only hope that the basin was emptied and refilled between Vikings!

Summertime soak

Keeping clean is very important to Vikings. When it's warm, a skinny-dip in a lake is a must. After that, a quick comb-through tackles hairy tangles and a poke with an ear spoon gets rid of any yucky wax.

Dudette fashion

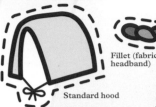

Peaked hood

Standard hood

Fillet (fabric headband)

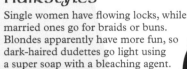

Hairstyles

Single women have flowing locks, while married ones go for braids or buns. Blondes apparently have more fun, so dark-haired dudettes go light using a super soap with a bleaching agent.

Headwear

There are scarves and hats a plenty to top off an outfit, from simple hoods to headbands.

Apron

A pair of bright brooches holds the apron to the dress.

Smock

When the cold creeps in, the chic chick stays snug with a smock on top of her outfit.

Key

Shawl

This wrap gives an extra layer of warmth and color, and is fastened with another brooch.

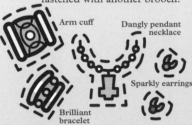

Arm cuff

Dangly pendant necklace

Sparkly earrings

Brilliant bracelet

Leather belt

Tiny tweezers

Pair of scissors

Hair comb

Jewelry

Viking women love glitzy, glam jewelry. The more money you have, the more jewelry you own.

Dudettes want to look good and take care of their appearance. Most women wear a long dress of linen or wool. Vikings go crazy for color and dye cloth with vegetable or mineral extracts. Dresses are topped with aprons. Leggings and leather shoes complete the outfit.

Ornate tools

Every task has a tool, and the Viking woman keeps the essentials pinned to her belt or hanging on a necklace, so they are always handy.

Steamy saunas

When the lakes freeze over, Vikings scrub up in a specially built heated bathhouse. Pouring water over a pile of super hot rocks makes the air inside all hot and steamy. Sweating it out in these saunas is a way of keeping squeaky clean without bathing.

Desirable dude

English dude John of Wallingford is sure the reason Viking men keep themselves so clean is to impress English women.

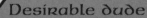

Ragnar Hairy-Breeches

Viking storytellers know that nothing keeps a crowd on the edge of their seats more than a ripping saga filled with heroic acts and daring deeds. This is a saga about Ragnar—a dude who finds out what a pain in the asp true love can be.

A jarl (nobleman) named Harraud gives his beautiful daughter, Thora, a pair of snakes as pets. She takes her pet-care duties a bit too seriously, overfeeding them so much they gobble a dead ox every day. Holy cow.

> Yummy...can I have sssssssome more?

Soon the supersized slitherers grow so large and strong that Thora is afraid to go near them, and so is everyone else. Harraud, desperate to get rid of the perilous pets (and none too happy about the food bill), proclaims that anyone who kills the snakes can marry his daughter. Thora is quite a babe, so many men try, but one after another, they fail.

> That dude's hisssstory.

One day, King Ragnar resolves to take up the challenge and win Thora's hand through cunning and skill. He puts on a coat and breeches made of thick, shaggy wool that is tough enough to resist snakebite. Then he sets off to do a little exterminating.

> Dude, this wool itches.

Ragnar plunges into a pool of ice-cold water. In an instant, his shaggy clothes freeze solid, making them even thicker and tougher to bite through. He really is one super-cool dude.

> Brrrring 'em on!

> Brrrr!

20

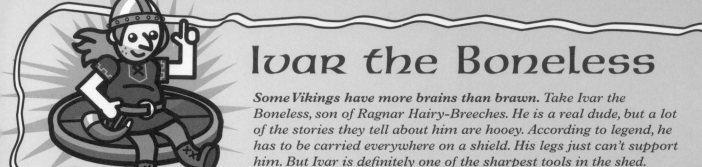

Ivar the Boneless

Some Vikings have more brains than brawn. Take Ivar the Boneless, son of Ragnar Hairy-Breeches. He is a real dude, but a lot of the stories they tell about him are hooey. According to legend, he has to be carried everywhere on a shield. His legs just can't support him. But Ivar is definitely one of the sharpest tools in the shed.

Ivar's dad, King Ragnar, launches one raid after another, amassing a great deal of wealth. One day he strikes out for the English kingdom of Northumbria, where King Ella pulls together an awesome army to crush Ragnar.

Many of Ragnar's men are slain and the great warrior himself is captured and chucked into a gruesome pit of deadly snakes. Before long the snakes slither over and bite him to death. That's venomous, dude.

Ragnar's sons, hell bent on revenge, head to England to battle Ella's men. Ivar's brothers fight with fury, but the English army is just too large and too tough. The weary brothers head back home.

Ivar has a plan. He asks King Ella to give him a plot of land to make up for killing his dad. He doesn't ask for much—just as much land as he can cover with an old bull hide.

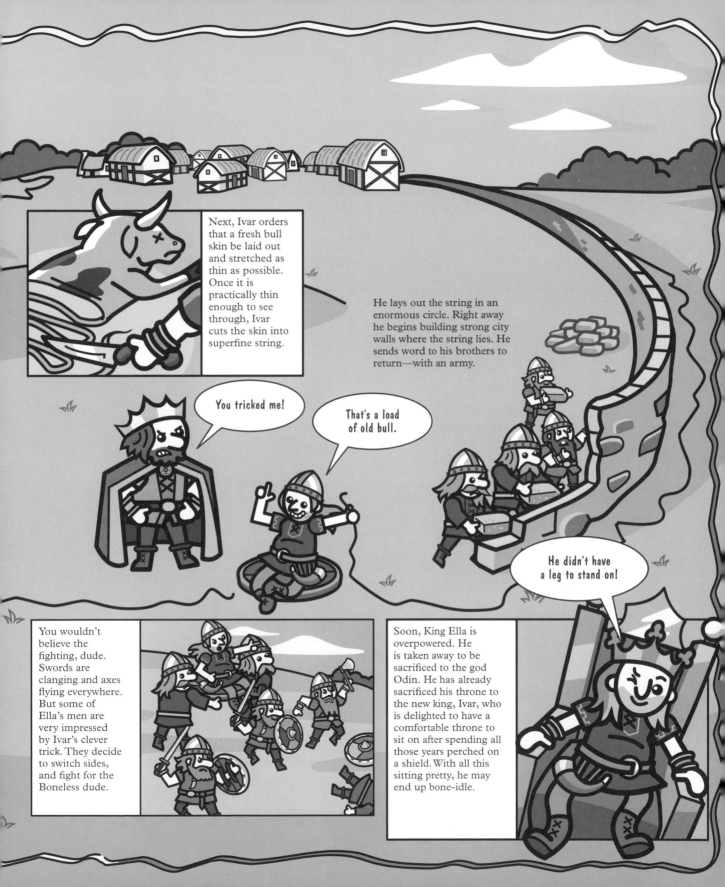

Next, Ivar orders that a fresh bull skin be laid out and stretched as thin as possible. Once it is practically thin enough to see through, Ivar cuts the skin into superfine string.

He lays out the string in an enormous circle. Right away he begins building strong city walls where the string lies. He sends word to his brothers to return—with an army.

You tricked me!

That's a load of old bull.

He didn't have a leg to stand on!

You wouldn't believe the fighting, dude. Swords are clanging and axes flying everywhere. But some of Ella's men are very impressed by Ivar's clever trick. They decide to switch sides, and fight for the Boneless dude.

Soon, King Ella is overpowered. He is taken away to be sacrificed to the god Odin. He has already sacrificed his throne to the new king, Ivar, who is delighted to have a comfortable throne to sit on after spending all those years perched on a shield. With all this sitting pretty, he may end up bone-idle.

Fun and games

All work and no play? Not the Vikings. Whenever dudes get together there is nothing they enjoy more than a good competitive game. Ball games, boardgames, tug-of-war, or skating—the Vikings know how to have fun. Whatever the weather, there's always something to play—and winning is the name of the game. (Vikings are bad losers.)

Top tugging

Take two tough teams, one ready rope, and plenty of pulling power—and you've got everything you need for a top game of tug-of-war. In one Viking variation, an animal skin replaces the rope. Sometimes the tug takes place over a blazing-hot fire. That puts a little tingle in your tug.

Trials of strength

Wrestling gives the more brutish dudes a chance to get rough. Grabbing each other by the arms or waists, wrestlers try to force their opponents off their feet and onto their backsides through sheer strength. Sometimes teams compete in wrestling matches, one arm-twisting pair at a time. The contests often result in broken bones.

Rocks and races

Foot races are a popular sport. To up the stakes a little, runners might carry heavy objects like armor or even giant rocks as they speed to the finish. Rocks are also handy for impromptu weight-lifting challenges. Dudes select a huge boulder and try to lift it over their shoulders. Massive muscles are a must to avoid a bash on the bonnet.

Dunking and diving

Swimming contests are a very popular spectator sport. Sometimes swimmers keep their armor or clothing on to make things tougher (if not rustier). The rules say that it's totally cool for a swimmer to drown his opponent. Now that's dirty pool.

Full board

The most popular boardgame is Hnefatafl—a strategy game, like chess. One player's pieces are a king and his guards, while the other player's are raiders, who try to capture the king. The board often rests on the players' knees. If a player stands up suddenly, it's back to square one.

Flip and grab

Knucklebones is a tricky test of reflexes, like jacks. Balance a pig or sheep bone on the back of the wrist, flip it into the air, grab another bone from a pile on the floor with the same hand, then catch the flipped bone before it lands. Not easy.

Having a ball

There are plenty of ball games to get stuck into. Balls are most often made of wood, but others are fashioned from leather. As with any contact sport, ball games can get a little out of hand. If you think a knock in the noggin from a wooden ball is a real headache, try having your ankle gnashed by a Viking.

On the hoof

Vikings don't just horse around with each other. Horse-fighting is wildly popular (especially betting on the results). Two horses are pitted against each other (within sight of a mare, to bring out their inner stallions), as their owners prod them with sticks. If an owner "happens" to use his stick on the wrong horse, then a rematch is demanded.

I knew I had the figure for skating.

Great skate

When the fjord freezes over, Vikings strap on skates—made from cow bones scraped until one side is flat and smooth—and hit the ice. They may play a hockey-like ball game as they glide along, or just skate for fun. Vikings also use skis, but for hunting expeditions, rather than for sport.

25

Rune master

Viking dudes have an awesome alphabet made up of symbols called runes. Each rune is like a stick figure with straight lines and sharp angles, making it easy to carve them into rocks and wood. Runes are said to have special powers, because they come from the god Odin. Many people can read and write runes, but only a few make magic with them. These are the rune masters, experts in spells and curses. Here's one of the magic dudes coming now.

Q: *Excuse me, oh rune master. Could you tell us about the runic alphabet? Love your work, by the way.*

A: Thanks, dude. See, the alphabet is called Futhark. It has 16 characters. We can write the letters in any direction—left to right, right to left, even up and down. That's probably why I have a permanent crick in my neck.

Q: *So how did Odin give the writing system to you?*

A: It's an awesome story. The legends say he speared himself to a tree, waiting for some sort of sacred message. After nine long days and nights of pretty much hanging around, he learned the mysteries of the runes and passed them on to his people.

Q: *Where can I see some Futhark?*

A: Well, people often mark household objects with runes to show who owns it. You know, like "Harald's horn." Warriors might carve the name of the god of war, Odin, into their swords or shields, so that he protects them and makes them stronger on the battlefield. Sometimes, when our creative juices are flowing, we write beautiful poems with the runes. Then there are the runestones— that's what I'm working on right now.

Q: *Dude, it's looking totally awesome. So what's the story with runestones?*

A: Most of these big slabs of rock carved with runes are monuments. They go up after someone dies as a memorial, to say a few nice words about the dude. Some people who are still alive put up a runestone to brag about something cool they've done.

> I'm glad I charge by the letter. It feels like I've been chiseling for days.

FUTHARK

26

Q: *Apart from carving runes, what else is in your job description? I hear that you are held in pretty high regard around here.*

A: That's true, dude. Here's the thing: lots of people can read and write runes, but not many understand how super powerful they are. After all, they're a gift from Odin, so they must be pretty divine, right? So, when dudes want a little fortune-telling, a magic spell, or even a nasty curse, they come knocking on my door.

Q: *Wow. How do you do that, man?*

A: Rune casting is popular. Say some dude comes to me with a big question about the future, I'm always ready to give a reading. I've got some pieces of bark carved with runic characters. I throw them on the ground, pick up three at random, then use those characters and my extra special mystical skills to find the answer. I've also got some awesome magic pebbles painted with runes. I shake them up in a leather pouch and pull out three to decide whether it's a yes or no answer. Cool, huh?

Q: *You said it. What about curses and spells and all that?*

A: The power is in the runes themselves—all I do is bring it into play. I can knock up a spell faster than you can say Futhark. You want a curse put on an enemy? I'm your dude.

Q: *One last question. Do you ever make a spelling mistake?*

A: Don't be cheeky with me, unless you want to find your life in runes…I mean ruins. Be off with you.

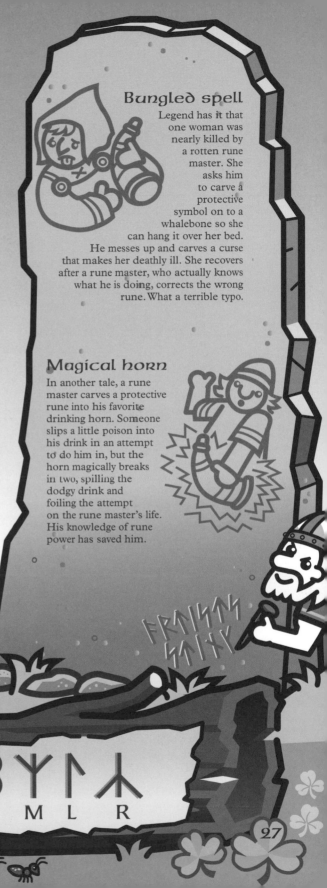

Bungled spell

Legend has it that one woman was nearly killed by a rotten rune master. She asks him to carve a protective symbol on to a whalebone so she can hang it over her bed. He messes up and carves a curse that makes her deathly ill. She recovers after a rune master, who actually knows what he is doing, corrects the wrong rune. What a terrible typo.

Magical horn

In another tale, a rune master carves a protective rune into his favorite drinking horn. Someone slips a little poison into his drink in an attempt to do him in, but the horn magically breaks in two, spilling the dodgy drink and foiling the attempt on the rune master's life. His knowledge of rune power has saved him.

H N I A S T B M L R

Find the island, my feathered friend.

Floki Raven

How do seafaring dudes know where they are going? Norwegian adventurer Floki has an unusual method of navigation: he lets ravens make the call. Is Floki one bird short of a flock? Not really. Ravens are land birds, not water birds. If they're hungry, they fly straight to land to find a snack. All Floki needs to do is follow.

Floki hears sailors talk about a vast island in the west called Snowland. He makes it his mission to go there, taking along three ravens, but no raven food. After two days, he lets one go, but it flies straight back home.

After a few more days heading due west, Floki releases the second hungry raven. It soars into the air, circles around the ship several times, then returns to the ship, completely wiped out.

That Floki dude is raven mad!

A couple of days later, the third raven is taken up to the deck. Dude, that bird is starving hungry. Floki sends it off, and it immediately takes a sharp turn to the northwest and disappears. Floki and his crew follow, and within 24 hours they are clambering out of the ship and strolling up to the shores of the fabled Snowland. (The raven, meanwhile, finds a rock he likes and puts a deposit on it.)

From that time on, Floki is known as Floki Raven. The new place really rocks. He and his crew settle down and things are good. But Floki somehow forgets that winter is just around the corner.

Cosmic cast

Viking mythology is full of amazing adventures starring a cast of gods and goddesses. Each god looks after a part of a Viking's daily life, from weather to warfare. Vikings believe that gods and regular dudes live in different worlds, all of them nestled in the branches of a huge tree called Yggdrasil (world tree). Its trunk grows through the human homes up to the land of the gods. Let's meet some of the dudes who've put down roots in this cosmic treehouse.

Asgard
Vikings call their gods Ases (stop giggling!) because they live in Asgard. Inside is Valhalla, a grand hall where warrior dudes who die in battle meet the gods.

Fire giants
The super-nasty fire giants live in a flaming-hot world. They terrify gods and humans alike, and will fight anything, except, obviously, fires.

Dark elves
The underground realm of Svartalfaheim is home to dark elves. They are great craftspeople, but they are also grumpy and moan a lot. Can't these dudes lighten up?

Midgard
Humans inhabit Midgard (Middle Earth), which is smack in the middle of Yggdrasil. The land is surrounded by ocean, where scary serpent Jormungand lives.

Niflheim
Ruled by Loki's daughter, Hel, this icy world is like a cosmic toll booth. Everyone must pass through. Most of the Viking dead end up here.

Dwarves
These little punks from Nidavellir are skilled magicians and blacksmiths. The only thing dwarves want to get their greedy mitts on is gold.

Light elves
The friendly elves of Alfheim have strange pale skin and are as tall as humans. With the right spells (and possibly sunblock) it is easy to keep them on your side.

Odin
God of war, wisdom, and magic, this dude is on a quest for knowledge. The bountifully bearded Odin travels the human world on an eight-legged horse. His ravens, Thought and Memory, fly ahead and report what they see. This awesome dude hangs his big floppy hat in Valhalla.

Thor
Muscle-bound Thor is one of the mightiest gods in Asgard. Guard of all the gods, Thor rides the skies in an iron cart pulled by two goats named Toothcracker and Toothgnasher. Thunder rumbles when his magical hammer Mjolnir (The Destroyer) is thrown. How heavy metal is that?

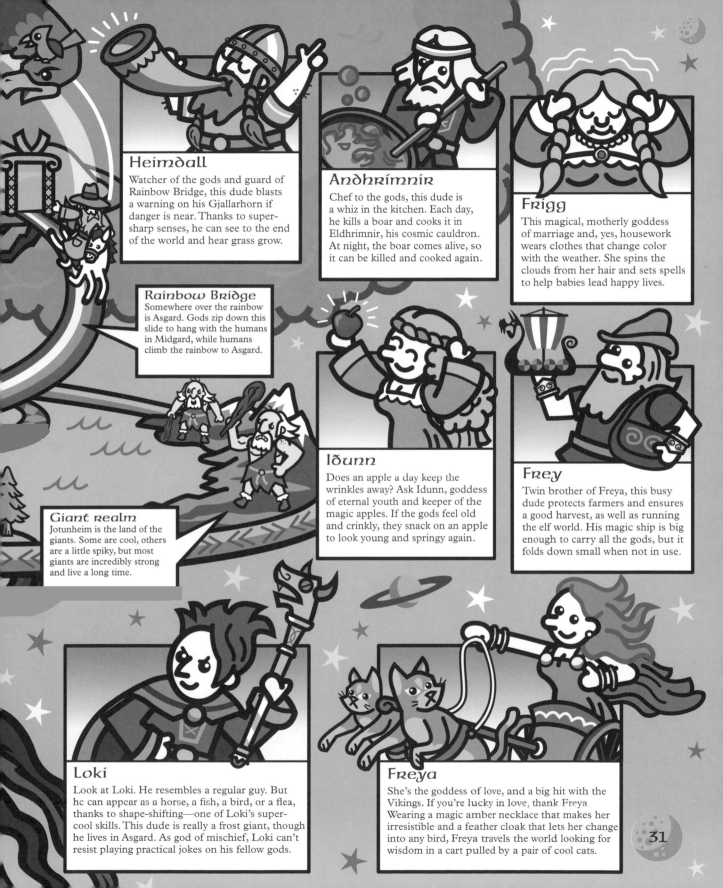

Heimdall

Watcher of the gods and guard of Rainbow Bridge, this dude blasts a warning on his Gjallarhorn if danger is near. Thanks to super-sharp senses, he can see to the end of the world and hear grass grow.

Andhrímnír

Chef to the gods, this dude is a whiz in the kitchen. Each day, he kills a boar and cooks it in Eldhrimnir, his cosmic cauldron. At night, the boar comes alive, so it can be killed and cooked again.

Frigg

This magical, motherly goddess of marriage and, yes, housework wears clothes that change color with the weather. She spins the clouds from her hair and sets spells to help babies lead happy lives.

Rainbow Bridge

Somewhere over the rainbow is Asgard. Gods zip down this slide to hang with the humans in Midgard, while humans climb the rainbow to Asgard.

Giant realm

Jotunheim is the land of the giants. Some are cool, others are a little spiky, but most giants are incredibly strong and live a long time.

Iðunn

Does an apple a day keep the wrinkles away? Ask Idunn, goddess of eternal youth and keeper of the magic apples. If the gods feel old and crinkly, they snack on an apple to look young and springy again.

Frey

Twin brother of Freya, this busy dude protects farmers and ensures a good harvest, as well as running the elf world. His magic ship is big enough to carry all the gods, but it folds down small when not in use.

Loki

Look at Loki. He resembles a regular guy. But he can appear as a horse, a fish, a bird, or a flea, thanks to shape-shifting—one of Loki's super-cool skills. This dude is really a frost giant, though he lives in Asgard. As god of mischief, Loki can't resist playing practical jokes on his fellow gods.

Freya

She's the goddess of love, and a big hit with the Vikings. If you're lucky in love, thank Freya. Wearing a magic amber necklace that makes her irresistible and a feather cloak that lets her change into any bird, Freya travels the world looking for wisdom in a cart pulled by a pair of cool cats.

The Theft of Thor's Hammer

The Vikings never tire of telling stories about their gods. Some are inspirational, some a little scary, and others downright silly. But all these tales will be handed down for future generations to enjoy. Here's one of the most famous yarns of yore: the tale of Thor and his missing hammer.

Loki tells him to chill and they head off to Freya's house. She has a magic feather robe that allows her to fly all over the place. Loki asks if he can borrow it, so he can zoom around and find the hammer. She agrees, and Loki sets off to the Land of the Giants.

> Try not to put too many miles on it, Loki.

Land of the Gods

One morning, Thor wakes up and reaches for the first thing he always does. No, not his bathrobe—his magic hammer. But where is it? He begins to shake as he fumbles around for it, but it's just not there. He races over to Loki, his shaggy beard all aquiver. "Dude! I have suffered a loss beyond perception. My HAMMER has been STOLEN!"

Land of the Giants

Loki lands bang in front of Thrym, the king of the frost giants, who is hanging with his dogs. Loki comes right out and asks him if he's the dude who took the hammer. "For sure, dude," Thrym says. "It's hidden eight leagues beneath the earth. And no one will get it from me unless he brings Freya here to be my bride." Loki flies back to the Land of the Gods.

Loki gives the scoop to Thor and Freya. Thor says, "You've heard the dude. You're getting married, and I'm getting my hammer back." But Freya is not happy. "I'd be crazy to agree to such a whacked-out plan as that," she protests.

Emergency meeting! All the gods gather to see if anyone has any bright ideas about how to get the hammer back. The god Heimdall has a brainwave. He tells Thor to put on one of Freya's fancy dresses, and accessorize with some bridal jewelry. Loki will travel with Thor back to the land of giants, disguised as "her" servant girl.

The wedding is officially off, dude.

A wedding feast is held in the Land of the Giants. The cross-dressing Thor eats his way through an entire ox. Thrym is shocked at how much his bride has consumed. Loki explains, "She's been so excited to marry you she hasn't eaten." Thrym tries to steal a kiss, and is surprised to find a pair of blazing eyes behind the bridal veil. "She been so excited that she hasn't slept either," Loki explains.

Thrym asks for the magic hammer, so he can offer it to his new bride. When Thor sees it, he tears off his bridal wear, seizes the hammer, and gives Thrym a thumping thwack. Then he gives all the giant's kin a good hammering.

So long, farewell

Vikings believe that after they die they will join the gods in the afterlife. The final farewell can be quite simple or a real humdinger. The send-off depends on your wealth and standing. Check out the burial rites for this dead chieftain. The dude's a great warrior and not short of a few bucks, so people are really pushing the boat out...before they set fire to it.

The dead dude is dressed in fine clothing and laid on a bed.

Servants may be killed to travel to the afterlife—surely not in the job description.

Horses are sometimes killed and put in the ship. Neigh way!

Valuables, such as jewelry, are packed up, too.

Elaborate burials take ages to prepare. The burial ship is loaded with everything the dead dude may need in the afterlife, then friends and family may kick-start the journey to the next world by setting the whole shebang alight. Later, a burial mound is built over the ashes. Other times, ships are set on fire and pushed out to sea. Sometimes Vikings skip the burning bit and just bury the ship under a mound of earth. Dudes without a ship can be buried under stones arranged

Furniture and trunks containing household goods go on the burial boat.

If this loyal dog makes it to the afterlife he may rethink that whole "man's best friend" thing.

A feast of food and drink is carried on board.

in a ship shape. Some Vikings bury the dead near the family home. While rich dudes are buried with luxuries, poor dudes are laid to rest with tools and utensils. People expect to be doing the same work in the next life, so they are prepared to be busy. Why the rush to the afterlife? Vikings believe that bravery in battle is rewarded after death. Female warriors take the heroes to Valhalla to live with the gods and enjoy fantastic feasts. The party never ends, dude.

Greetings from Hedeby

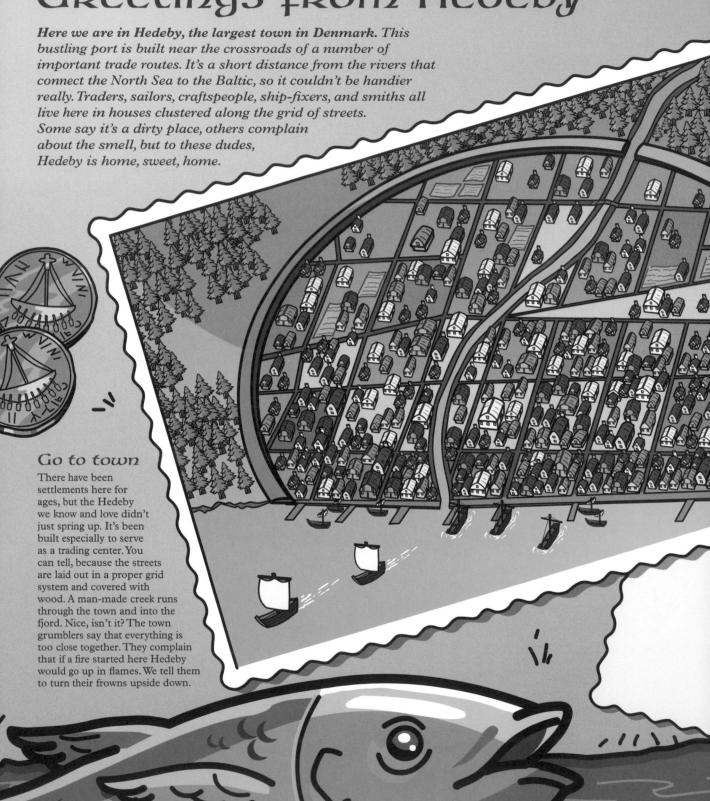

Here we are in Hedeby, the largest town in Denmark. This bustling port is built near the crossroads of a number of important trade routes. It's a short distance from the rivers that connect the North Sea to the Baltic, so it couldn't be handier really. Traders, sailors, craftspeople, ship-fixers, and smiths all live here in houses clustered along the grid of streets. Some say it's a dirty place, others complain about the smell, but to these dudes, Hedeby is home, sweet, home.

Go to town

There have been settlements here for ages, but the Hedeby we know and love didn't just spring up. It's been built especially to serve as a trading center. You can tell, because the streets are laid out in a proper grid system and covered with wood. A man-made creek runs through the town and into the fjord. Nice, isn't it? The town grumblers say that everything is too close together. They complain that if a fire started here Hedeby would go up in flames. We tell them to turn their frowns upside down.

Busy, busy, busy

There are trading posts aplenty in Hedeby, as well as workshops where ironworkers, carpenters, weavers, metal smiths, and leatherworkers are hard at work. People live in fenced-off, rectangular plots of land along the streets. Each plot has a main house as well as outbuildings, maybe a well, and hopefully a latrine.

Reassuring rampart

A semicircular rampart (a wall of timber and earth) surrounds the town and protects its dudes. The only way to get to town is via two entrance gates or from the harbor. The town sourpuss says there's nothing worth protecting here, but we beg to differ.

Wish you were here?

Many dudes pass through our lovely town on the way from here to there. It's always been that way, and probably always will. While we are very happy to welcome them, and our merchants are certainly grateful for the business, some people don't quite warm to the place as we do. Just look at what Arab traveler Ibrahim Al-Tartushi had to say about our beloved city. To each his own, we say. Don't let the rampart door hit you on your way out.

Hi Mom,

Here I am in a bummer of a town called Hedeby. There's nothing to do and the locals get by on next to no funds. I've seen people throw their kids in the sea to save bucks. Everyone eats fish, which was yummy at first, but when the whole town stinks of smelly salmon, the novelty wears off pretty quick. Dudettes have the right to divorce, so I guess the dudes avoid commitment. Eye make-up is all the rage, the style is to keep slapping it on. Even dudes wear it—shocker. My biggest bother is the constant singing. These dudes are tone-deaf, yet they won't can it. I'm checking out of here while my ears still work.

Can't wait to get home,

Ibrahim

Harald the Shaggy

An heir with some serious hair issues, Harald's tangled tale begins in A.D. 850, in a small Norwegian kingdom ruled by his dad, Halfdan the Black. One night, Harald's mom has a weird dream in which her son is a tree with branches that grow until they wrap around Norway. Will Harald live up to this prophecy and conquer the country?

Later, dad dude.

No one is sure why, but King Harald makes a vow: he will not let his hair be cut or even combed until he conquers all of Norway. Scissors and combs rust all over Vestfold, and hairy Harald soon finds himself with a new nickname— Harald the Shaggy.

When Harald is just ten years old, his father drowns—a major downer for the little dude. Young Harald inherits the throne of Vestfold, his father's kingdom on the coast of southern Norway.

Begone with your beauty treatments!

Bound by his vow and unbothered by his big, bad hair, Harald the Shaggy begins his fight for Norway in A.D. 866. First stop are the kingdoms next door. Harald barges in on his neighbors, battles their armies, and conquers their lands. Soon, the territory the hairy dude controls is growing as quickly as his fierce flowing locks.

This battle is a close shave... not that I'd know.

With many kingdoms now under his hairy thumb, Harald cuts a deal with a rival king in the Uplands, then his army runs amok across the country, warring their way north toward Throndheim. With each victory, Harald wins more goodies to reward his band of baddies. The dude even has tunes that brag about his exploits. Singing poets called skalds flock to Harald's side, writing songs about his good fortune (very important to Vikings) and bravery. But not everyone is impressed...

THRONDHEIM

UPLANDS

VESTFOLD

Harald has made plenty of enemies who would like their lands back. As he sets sail with a fleet to finish his conquest, a dude name Solvi Bandy-legs escapes. His plan is to go to nearby kingdoms and ask for help.

King dudes, we must unite and fight!

Bandy-legs bends the ears of several kings and jarls who are already pretty fed up with Harald. They want their freedom and they are willing to fight for it. They gather a wicked crew of warriors, load up their ships with as many weapons as they can grab, and hit the waves to meet Harald's fleet head-on. Harald gets wind of what's happening and lies in wait. It's all looking very hairy indeed. When the ships meet, a gigantic sea battle follows. Swords, spears, and shields clash and clang as whole ships are cleared of warriors. In the end, one man stands head and shoulders (and hair) above the fray. Harald the Shaggy has won his toughest battle, and Norway is his.

Hurry up and give in, my stylist is waiting.

Just ten years, or 3,650 bad hair days, after making his vow, Harald the Shaggy is ready for his makeover. Harald's lovely locks earn him a new nickname: Harald Fairhair.

I feel ten years younger.

Rollo
of Normandy

Many Viking raiders strike their targets, plunder the goodies, and move on to the next town. Others decide to stick around. Meet Rollo—nicknamed "the Walker," either because the dude's so tall that when he sits on his horse he looks like he's walking, or because he's just too big for any horse to carry. Here's the story of how he walked all over the opposition in France.

Rollo is not crazy about living under Harald Fairhair's rule, so he sets off with his band (known as Northmen) to attack northwestern France.

In 911, Rollo lays siege to Chartres, a town about 60 miles (94 km) from Paris. The onslaught is brutal, dude. The French king, Charles the Simple, faces a tricky choice. He can either pay Rollo a huge amount of money to go away and leave Chartres alone, or he can strike some kind of deal with the lanky leader.

King Charles comes up with a cool plan to not only stop the fighting, but also to prevent future attacks. He offers a peace treaty to Rollo, and promises to give the Vikings a large chunk of land around the town of Rouen, but there is a catch. And it's a doozy.

Rollo must agree to defend and protect the land from other Viking raids. Seems fair enough. He must also swear his loyalty to the king and convert to his Christian religion. No surprises there. But here is the kicker: in order to seal the deal, Rollo must kiss the king on the foot. He absolutely refuses and orders one of his men to do the deed.

You've really put your foot in it now, dude!

This dastardly dude lifts King Charles's foot to his mouth, puckers up, then at the very last second gives the twinkle-toed king a shove that sends him tumbling to the ground. But soon things get back on an even footing. Rollo stays true to the terms of the treaty and defends his new territory. The region becomes known as the home of the Northmen, or Normandy.

J'taime. May I kiss your toes?

Rollo and his men move into Normandy. They marry French wives who teach them the local lingo, and gradually settle down. The Walker has found a place where he can put his feet up and rest his long legs.

Here's the Thing

In Iceland they have this thing, dude. Every summer, Icelanders join together to do their thing at the Thing. The Thing is an enormous gathering of all the free people in the land. There are so many big things happening at the Thing—it really is something to see. Let's take a look.

What's the Thing?

All the big decisions of the day are discussed at the Thing. For example, if two families are feuding, they've got to sort it out at the Thing. If someone has murdered another person, the people at the Thing decide what kind of punishment is deserved. Getting things out in the open at the Thing is a good way to keep law and order in society.

Vikings with issues

Dudes come to the Thing to air their issues. In theory, everyone has an equal voice (although the rich tend to have a bigger say in things). That's the way Things go.

Lawspeaker

This clever old dude knows all the laws off by heart. He recites them for everybody at the Thing.

Setting up shelter

Temporary homes and stalls are built with boulders or chunks of sod, topped with wooden frames covered in fabric.

Who runs the Thing?

The whole Thing is overseen by the lawspeakers. These dudes are like a cross between a judge and the chairperson of a meeting. They ensure things at the Thing run smoothly, keep the peace, and make sure everyone follows the rules. Lawspeakers have totally memorized all the laws that have been decided before. Now that's something.

Who goes?

In addition to the lawspeakers and chieftains, dudes from all over the country flock to the Thing—it's pretty packed. The Thing is held in the same place every year. Everyone who has issues to discuss comes along, but the Thing is also a great place to do a little trading, arrange marriages, and just hang out, let your hair down, and have fun.

What happens there?

It's a festive atmosphere. There are beer brewers and food stands selling munchies to the guests, and plenty of other merchants hawking their goods, from sword sharpeners to rune masters offering spells. There's even entertainment. So, while the people at the Thing have important decisions to make, they also have a wicked cool time.

In thing

The Thing really is the place to be. Leaders from foreign lands, people looking for work, and even beggars hoping for handouts all make their way to the Thing.

Buy something

From trinkets to treasure, there's something for everyone at the Thing.

Harald Bluetooth

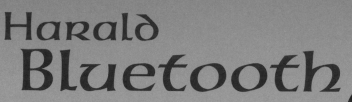

Word of mouth says King Harald Bluetooth is about to make Viking history. Harald is king of Denmark and his sister, widow of the Norwegian king Erik Blood Axe, asks for help in ruling Norway. He sees his chance and ends up ruler of both countries by 960. But has Bluetooth bitten off more than he can chew? Let's ask the man of the molar, sorry, moment.

Q: *Ooops! I didn't know you were in the bath. Please excuse me. I'll try again later.*

A: Silly goose, I'm not in the bath. I'm being baptized. It's a ritual necessary to join the Christian faith. This priest is pouring water over me to wash away my sins, as well as some stuff that got stuck in my mustache, and welcome me to the faith. We'll need a bigger tub because the Danes are going to become Christians, too. Not that they have a say in the matter.

God vs. gods

We're sitting around at dinner. The conversation gets pretty hot—are the Viking gods stronger than the Christian one? Bishop Poppo thinks our gods are really demons. I devise a test to decide.

Testing, testing

I ask Poppo if he's willing to put his faith to the test. He agrees immediately. I tell him that I'm going to stick a piece of iron in the fire until it is absolutely red hot.

What a handful

It's unbelievable. Poppo holds the sizzling hot iron in his hand as proof of his faith. I keep waiting for him to drop it and run away screaming, but he never lets go.

Holy moly

This is the best bit. When Poppo lets go of the iron, there isn't a mark on his hand. Right then and there, I decide to side with the big "G."

Q: *So the rumors are true. How did this happen? Haven't Christians been trying to convert Danish dudes for ages?*

A: Yes, indeed. The Church has been sending missionaries since about 700, but up until recently I haven't been too impressed. We are very happy with the gods and goddesses we already have, thank you very much. But then something amazing happened. Look into my thoughts, and you will see.

Q: *That's pretty convincing stuff. But do you think it's enough to convert an entire nation?*

A: Tough call. Paganism has been the religion of choice for centuries. My own parents were pagans. Mom was as pagan as pagan can be. Dad was devoted to Odin and did everything to stop other religions from spreading. It's a big world, so maybe there's room for Christianity, too. I'm looking forward to better relations with the Christian kings of Germany.

Q: *I hear you're making changes at your folks' graves at Jelling in Jutland, Denmark. Any chance of a preview?*

A: Mom and Dad were buried there in a pagan ceremony, so I'm going to build a church and move them inside. I'll put up a runestone in their memory, but I'm planning on using some Christian drawings, too. That will show people I'm serious about my new faith, and remind them I'm the king around here, dude. Enough questions. Back to the baptism.

Greenland

Eric the Red has a little problem: he's been outlawed from Norway after a spot of bother... well, a double murder, actually—and now he's been kicked out of the Thing at Iceland for killing again. Guess he saw red. Anyway, the red-headed, red-bearded dude needs a new home, pronto. (He also needs to stop killing people, but let's worry about somewhere to live first.)

An outlaw again, Eric wonders where to go. He's heard about a land to the west that was spotted about 50 years earlier. Not having much choice in the matter, the fiery dude sails off solo to try to find it.

Eric reaches the new land. It's not at all bad. No one seems to be there, so he sets out exploring the place on his own. For three years he travels around his new home.

Eric grows to like the place. He names the mountains and lakes. Sure, it is icy in spots, but there are excellent grassy areas around the fjord. They look like super sites for farms.

There are animals everywhere to catch and eat. It seems they've never seen people before. You can walk right up to them and get them (it doesn't seem fair, but a man has to eat.)

When the three years is up, Eric's outlaw status runs out and he can come back to Iceland. He tells everyone all about the amazing place he's found. He describes a land of great natural beauty and incredible bounty. He thinks he'd better give the place an attractive name, to draw in potential settlers. He goes for Eric. No, actually, he names it Greenland. Sounds lush.

x3

Eric's got good timing. Lots of people are itching to leave Iceland because the best bits have been taken. In the year 985, he takes 25 large ships, loaded up with settlers, animals, weapons, tools, and supplies, and sets off for Greenland. Everything you need to settle a new country is jammed on board.

The journey is not an easy one, with only 14 ships making it as far as Greenland. Some ships are forced to turn back, while others get crushed by wild waves in rough storms.

At the final passenger count, about 450 dudes are left on what little remains of the fleet. Most people are relieved when they see the coast of Greenland.

A few dudes are less keen on their early glimpses of Greenland and grumble to Eric that they can't see the green bits. The hot-headed dude shakes with anger at the ungrateful bunch. Relocations are never easy.

The dudes establish colonies on the coast, but it takes time to make the new settlements work and life is a struggle. Eventually the colonies flourish and everyone agrees that Greenland is a great land.

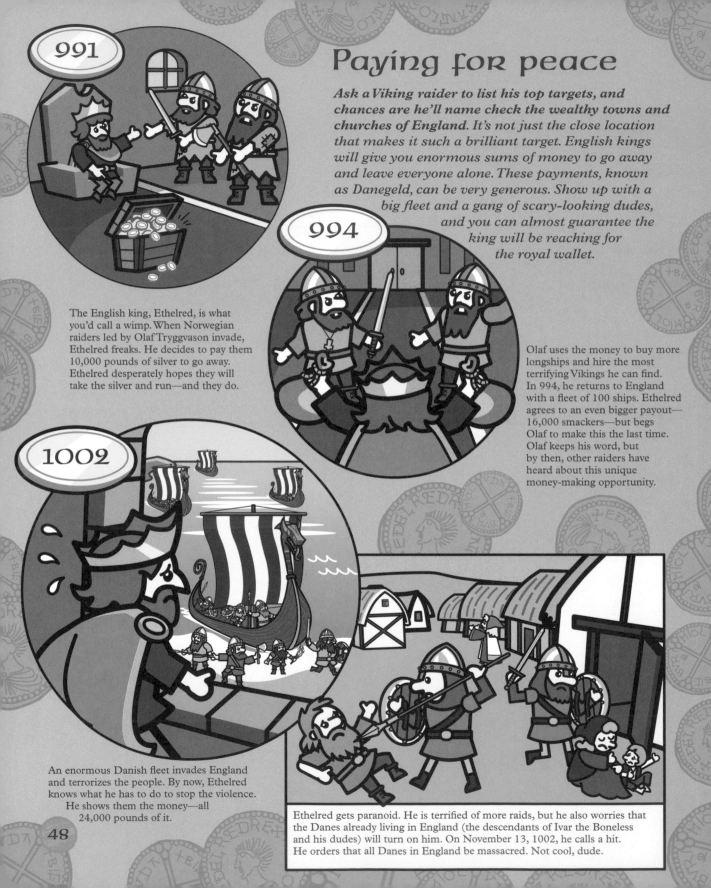

Paying for peace

991

Ask a Viking raider to list his top targets, and chances are he'll name check the wealthy towns and churches of England. It's not just the close location that makes it such a brilliant target. English kings will give you enormous sums of money to go away and leave everyone alone. These payments, known as Danegeld, can be very generous. Show up with a big fleet and a gang of scary-looking dudes, and you can almost guarantee the king will be reaching for the royal wallet.

The English king, Ethelred, is what you'd call a wimp. When Norwegian raiders led by Olaf Tryggvason invade, Ethelred freaks. He decides to pay them 10,000 pounds of silver to go away. Ethelred desperately hopes they will take the silver and run—and they do.

994

Olaf uses the money to buy more longships and hire the most terrifying Vikings he can find. In 994, he returns to England with a fleet of 100 ships. Ethelred agrees to an even bigger payout—16,000 smackers—but begs Olaf to make this the last time. Olaf keeps his word, but by then, other raiders have heard about this unique money-making opportunity.

1002

An enormous Danish fleet invades England and terrorizes the people. By now, Ethelred knows what he has to do to stop the violence. He shows them the money—all 24,000 pounds of it.

Ethelred gets paranoid. He is terrified of more raids, but he also worries that the Danes already living in England (the descendants of Ivar the Boneless and his dudes) will turn on him. On November 13, 1002, he calls a hit. He orders that all Danes in England be massacred. Not cool, dude.

1006

The Danish fleet returns and demands another payout. Ethelred hands over 36,000 pounds of silver, but wonders if the whole Danegeld thing is such a good idea.

For a couple of years, things calm down. Ethelred weighs up his options. He decides to build up a large English fleet at the coastal town of Sandwich, to defend England against the Viking raiders. They'll be back...he knows they will. This time, he'll be ready.

By 1009, Ethelred has more ships than any English king has ever had. The fleet is ready for anything—except maybe the weather. Many of the ships are destroyed when a big storm blows in, and others are lost in a minor battle. Ethelred is truly up the creek without a paddle now.

Danish ruler King Sweyn leads an invasion to England in 1013 with his son, Canute. The place is a shambles. Ethelred has no silver left to buy off the Vikings, so he runs away. King Sweyn takes control of the whole country. Result!

Leif Erikson

Nicknamed Leif the Lucky, this awesome dude is a born explorer. You've heard of his father Erik the Red who explored and settled Greenland. Well, they say the apple doesn't fall far from the tree, and that's certainly true in this family. Young Leif is soon off on his own amazing voyage of discovery, where he comes across a land of grapes and calls it Vineland. Later on, another explorer changes the name to America, but Leif's already been and gone. Lucky him—he got first dibs with the grapes.

One day, Leif spots a busted-up ship rowing past. On board is Bjarni Hergelfson, who says he got lost on a trip to Greenland and discovered an unknown tree-covered land.

Leif buys Bjarni's ship and sets sail in search of the mystery land. After sailing around Greenland, he goes west. He eventually reaches a rocky land of glaciers in the Canadian Arctic. Wrong.

Heading south, Leif discovers sandy beaches and trees. It's the north coast of Canada and he names it Woodland. Leif decides to keep exploring to see what other lands are waiting to be found.

He continues to wind his way south and two days later reaches an island, just off a larger mainland. This mainland looks like the best place yet.

The forest is incredibly lush, the land is unbelievably rich, and the salmon are enormous compared with the fish back at home. Leif's feeling lucky now. He uses some of the local wood to build a house, then he and his men start checking the place out.

One group of dudes heads into the forest, but when they return, they are missing one of their number, a German called Tyrker. They send out a search party and scour the island. The next morning, they find the missing dude.

Tyrker can't stop grinning. He's clearly excited and very eager to tell everyone about the amazing discovery he's made: grapes, huge clusters of the juicy fruit hanging from the forest vines.

Leif orders his men to load their ships with grapes, vines, and felled trees. In the spring they travel home, with tales of the place Leif calls Vineland. (That isn't bad. It could have been Salmonland.)

Alright, alright! I'm leaving!

A few years later, Leif's brother Thorvald returns to Vineland, planning to set up a colony there. What he doesn't realize is that there are loads of people there already—the Native Americans. They don't exactly welcome Thorvald with open arms, and he abandons his plan pretty sharpish.

Viking trade

Raiding villages and taking the good stuff can be very profitable, but it's not exactly a steady source of income. For that, Vikings rely on trade. They load their ships or wagons with stuff they have plenty of and travel along busy trade routes that spread across Europe and beyond, to swap their cargo for local goods. They ply their wares all over the place, from small trading outposts in remote areas to bustling market towns jam-packed with shoppers and swappers. Things change hands faster than you can say, "sold!"

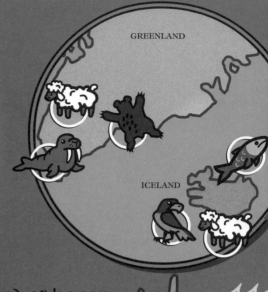

GREENLAND

ICELAND

Land of honey

Traders with a sweet tooth buzz off to England for the honey. This is also the number one destination for wool, silver, tin, and wheat. The town of Jorvik (York) is one of the biggest trading towns around. Over in Ireland, the city of Dublin is the center for the slave trade.

KEY

 Fish
A large catch can net a huge profit

 Furs
Fox, bear, deer, and elk are popular pelts

 Wine
Vikings brew beer but must import wine

 Ivory
Tusk, tusk…walrus tusks make ivory

 Swords
Prices rarely slashed on these weapons

 Falcons
Bag a bird or two and take them hunting

 Horses
At these prices, you can't say neigh

 Timber
Vikings log on here for wood

 Honey
This sweet stuff is the bee's knees

 Slaves
Lots of victims to choose from

 Jewelry
Come and buy your bling here

 Silk
Smooth cloth made from worm cocoons

 Silver
A sturdy, durable, and valuable metal

Wool
Fluffy fabric made from sheep's hair

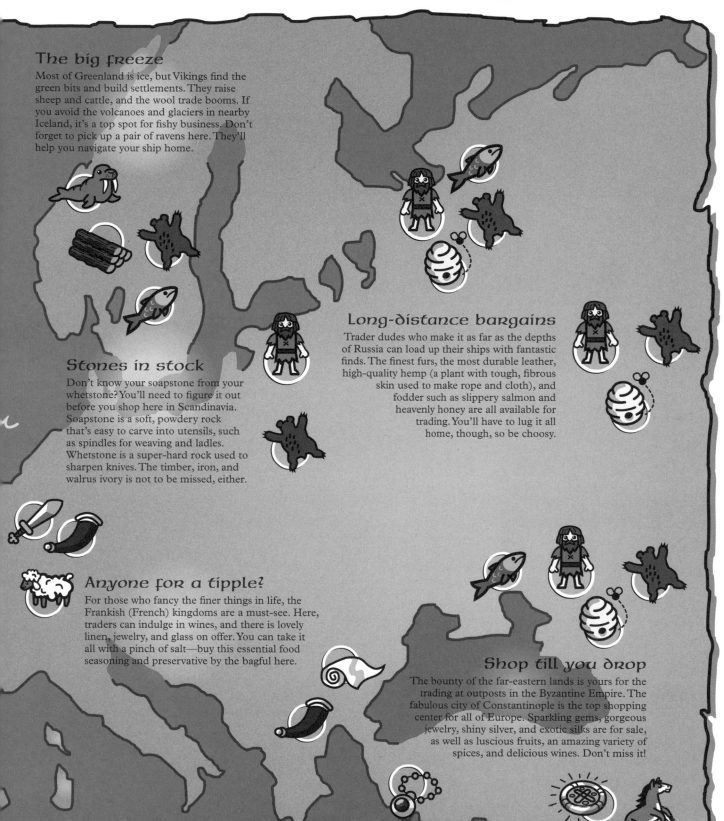

The big freeze

Most of Greenland is ice, but Vikings find the green bits and build settlements. They raise sheep and cattle, and the wool trade booms. If you avoid the volcanoes and glaciers in nearby Iceland, it's a top spot for fishy business. Don't forget to pick up a pair of ravens here. They'll help you navigate your ship home.

Stones in stock

Don't know your soapstone from your whetstone? You'll need to figure it out before you shop here in Scandinavia. Soapstone is a soft, powdery rock that's easy to carve into utensils, such as spindles for weaving and ladles. Whetstone is a super-hard rock used to sharpen knives. The timber, iron, and walrus ivory is not to be missed, either.

Long-distance bargains

Trader dudes who make it as far as the depths of Russia can load up their ships with fantastic finds. The finest furs, the most durable leather, high-quality hemp (a plant with tough, fibrous skin used to make rope and cloth), and fodder such as slippery salmon and heavenly honey are all available for trading. You'll have to lug it all home, though, so be choosy.

Anyone for a tipple?

For those who fancy the finer things in life, the Frankish (French) kingdoms are a must-see. Here, traders can indulge in wines, and there is lovely linen, jewelry, and glass on offer. You can take it all with a pinch of salt—buy this essential food seasoning and preservative by the bagful here.

Shop till you drop

The bounty of the far-eastern lands is yours for the trading at outposts in the Byzantine Empire. The fabulous city of Constantinople is the top shopping center for all of Europe. Sparkling gems, gorgeous jewelry, shiny silver, and exotic silks are for sale, as well as luscious fruits, an amazing variety of spices, and delicious wines. Don't miss it!

START & FINISH

NORWAY

Thorgil and his dudes rock up to the dock and load up the knarr with their cargo. He double-checks that he's got his set of scales to measure out the silver. A final farewell, and they're off.

WHALE

Blubbering blowholes! A whale is surfacing under the ship! It's a whale of a story for the dudes back home.

FOG

The weather is working against Thorgil. His ship hits heavy fog. It's impossible to see anything out there. He must wait until the fog lifts before he can get home.

MR. FIX-IT

Thorgil has to make an unscheduled stop, and spend some silver on new wood to fix up the ship.

Trader and ship

Meet Thorgil the Trader. Clock the cloak and fuzzy fur hat! The dude's obviously doing well for himself. He sails on a knarr, a wooden ship wider and deeper than a longship, so there's plenty of room for cargo. The boat gets its power from the wind pushing the sails.

Traders

Are you a wheeler-dealer in the making? Are you a marketplace master? Could you sell ice cubes to Icelanders? If you've got a head for business, an eye for a bargain, a nose for a good deal—and the stomach for a long but lucrative trip up and down the trade routes—you're ready to try your luck as the ultimate traveling salesman: the Viking trader. Your mission is to sail to Iceland and Ireland, making deals all the way. If you fail, the whole trip's a washout, and you're back to square one, dude.

Slaves and cargo

Four male slaves power the oars at the front and back of the ship. (Told you Thorgil is loaded—not everyone can afford slaves.) On this trip, Thorgil is taking a load of timber and walrus ivory out to trade. He's hoping to snap up something really valuable when he's out there—maybe a hunting bird like this one. Ready? Let's sail.

SINKING FAST

Thorgil heads home, heavier in cargo. Maybe too heavy...the ship springs a leak.

DUBLIN

Just as the other trader predicts, the birds are a hit at the market in Dublin. Thorgil gets a chunk of change and has his pick of the slaves.

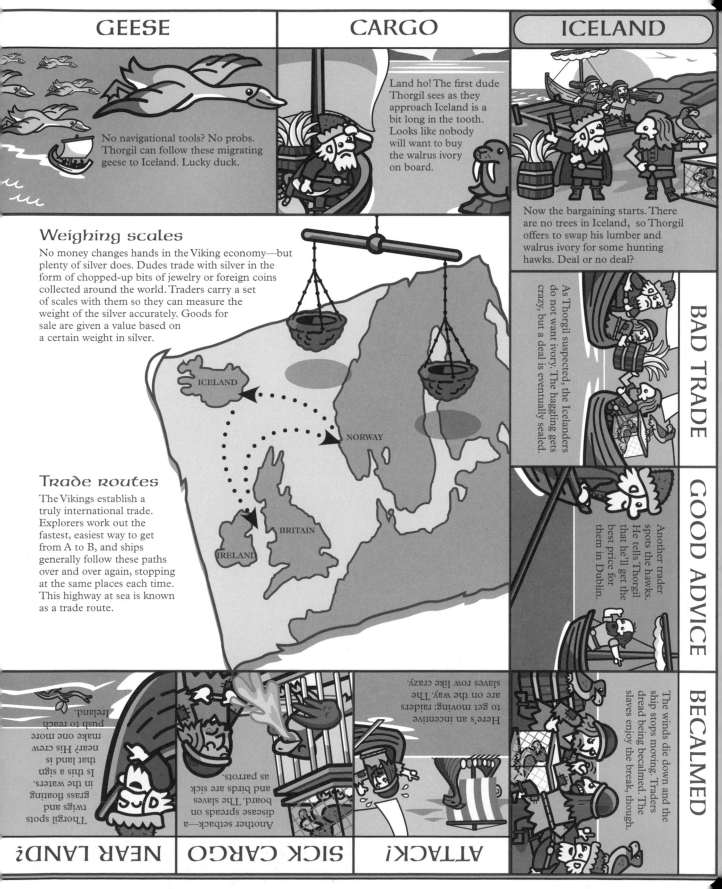

GEESE

No navigational tools? No probs. Thorgil can follow these migrating geese to Iceland. Lucky duck.

CARGO

Land ho! The first dude Thorgil sees as they approach Iceland is a bit long in the tooth. Looks like nobody will want to buy the walrus ivory on board.

ICELAND

Now the bargaining starts. There are no trees in Iceland, so Thorgil offers to swap his lumber and walrus ivory for some hunting hawks. Deal or no deal?

Weighing scales

No money changes hands in the Viking economy—but plenty of silver does. Dudes trade with silver in the form of chopped-up bits of jewelry or foreign coins collected around the world. Traders carry a set of scales with them so they can measure the weight of the silver accurately. Goods for sale are given a value based on a certain weight in silver.

Trade routes

The Vikings establish a truly international trade. Explorers work out the fastest, easiest way to get from A to B, and ships generally follow these paths over and over again, stopping at the same places each time. This highway at sea is known as a trade route.

Map labels: ICELAND, NORWAY, BRITAIN, IRELAND

BAD TRADE

As Thorgil suspected, the Icelanders do not want ivory. The haggling gets crazy, but a deal is eventually sealed.

GOOD ADVICE

Another trader spots the hawks. He tells Thorgil that he'll get the best price for them in Dublin.

BECALMED

The winds die down and the ship stops moving. Traders dread being becalmed. The slaves enjoy the break, though.

ATTACK!

Here's an incentive to get moving: raiders are on the way. The slaves row like crazy.

SICK CARGO

Another setback—a disease spreads on board. The slaves and birds are sick as parrots.

NEAR LAND?

Thorgil spots twigs and grass floating in the waters. Is this a sign that land is near? His crew make one more push to reach Ireland.

Going east

To the east of the Viking lands, across the Baltic Sea, lies the vast wilderness of Russia. The woods here are chockablock with animals whose coats are one of the most valuable goods for trade. Vikings sail Russia's rivers, taking furs to swap for silk, spices, and exotic goods from other towns. As well as trading, they do a little raiding. Well, they are Vikings.

Small ships

The Russian rivers are no place for the biggest Viking ships that sail the Atlantic—they'll get stuck, dude. Traders rely on small boats, no more than 40 ft (12 m) in length. Boats are built to be lightweight and flexible, because they take a bashing on the river rocks.

Rocks and rapids

During a single trading trip, bold Vikings could cover nearly 2,000 miles (3,218 km). On the plus side, most of the journey can be made by river, but the bad news is the river throws up some hazards. With a rocky riverbed, rapids to ride, and waterfalls—it's one crazy trip.

Setting up shop

Many of the Viking visitors like what they see in the new lands and decide to settle there. Dudes set up trading posts or one-stop shops where traders can fix their boats or load up on supplies before venturing out again into the wild. Some of these new settlers make a very good living here.

Portage

What happens when the river narrows or even runs out? You've got to get out, unload your stuff, pick it and the boat up, and move to the next river on foot. This is called portage, and it's one tough gig. Some settlements spring up near major portage sites. The dudes who live there will help you haul your gear…for a price.

Come to Kiev

Some smart dudes set up a trading base in a place called Kiev. The town isn't much to write home about—the locals are always up for a fight and the rapid-rammed river tosses ships around like rubber ducks in a tub. But the location's ideal for catching traders about to head across the Black Sea, and they do a mean chicken kiev.

Are we there yet?

Crossing the wilderness is a daunting task. It's a long, weary journey through dense forests, soupy swamps, and large grassy plains—not to mention the hungry bears. It really takes it out of a dude, and only the toughest, cleverest, and most ruthless survive. Memorial stones record the names of those who don't make it.

Riches over the water

Imagine dragging your butt all the way across Russia and then finding out that there was one more leg to your journey: the 500-mile (804-km) voyage across the Black Sea. Well, you mustn't grumble. On the other side of the Black Sea is the biggest and richest city in Europe—Constantinople, which Vikings call Miklagard, meaning "the great city."

Spoilt for choice

The city of Constantinople is certainly a sight to behold. It's huge—some people say there are half a million dudes there—and you won't believe the good stuff you get for a couple of furs. The finest silks, beautiful silver, and incredible sweet-smelling spices: definitely a happy ending to an epic journey.

57

Harald Hardrada

Epic travels, mad battlefield tactics, the death of a king under mysterious circumstances, and burning birds: the dude they call the Hard Ruler, Harald Hardrada, certainly lives a life full of adventure. His story begins at age 15, when he fights alongside his big bro, King Olaf of Norway. Olaf dies on the battlefield, and a wounded Harald rounds up a group of loyal warriors and flees to Russia.

Harald joins forces with Russia's King Jaroslav. But Harald is restless and sets his sights on Constantinople—the richest city in the world.

Constantinople

There, Harald joins the Varangian Guard, the emperor's special ops force. A born leader, Harald rises through the ranks and uses his top-dog position to do a few raids on the side. Nothing gets in his way. When he can't break into a castle, he catches birds, attaches wood shavings to them, and sets them alight. The birds fly into the castle, the castle burns, and Harald gets the goods.

Maria, the niece of the empress, catches his eye. He asks for her hand in marriage, but the answer is a flat no. The empress says Harald hasn't been sharing the booty from his raids fairly and throws him in the clink.

You don't share the goods, you don't get the girl.

Harald makes a daring escape from prison. He captures Maria, rouses his men, steals a ship in the harbor, and rows out to sea. But there is one more hurdle to overcome... and it's a big one.

The harbor is protected with a thick chain that stops boats from coming in and out. When they reach it, Harald comes up with a crazy idea that just might work. He orders everyone who is not rowing to run to the back of the boat, so their combined weight makes the bow (the front of the boat) tip up. He tells the dudes with the oars to row for their lives. Amazingly, the ship begins to climb up the chain.

When the ship is almost over the chain, Harald orders everyone to the bow. The ship tips forward into the open seas. Harald releases Maria with a message for the empress—no one controls Harald the Hard.

Harald marries his old mate King Jaroslav's daughter, and decides to take his new wife (and his massive fortune) back to Norway. The Norwegian king, Magnus, is threatened by this powerful new arrival. He agrees to rule alongside him.

Just a year later, Magnus lies dead and Harald is the one and only king. What happened to Magnus? No one really knows...except maybe Harald.

Who rules?

It is January 1066 and the English king Edward the Confessor dies after a 23-year reign. His death triggers a deadly struggle between three dudes to seize the crown. The royal council names Harold Godwinson king, but that doesn't stop the other contenders.

Harold Godwinson

Round one

Round two

Edward's brother-in-law Harold is the most powerful dude in England.

King Harold knows that two other dudes are on their way to claim the crown. He sends his friends Edwin and Morcar to defend the north, and prepares his fleet in the south.

Harold hears that Harald is in England. He gathers an army and heads toward York. They make the nearly 200-mile (300-km) trip in just five days. Dude, we're talking ASAP here.

King Harald Hardrada

A scheming Norwegian king with his eye on the prize—England.

Harald Hardrada's claim is a bit dodgy (he swears blind that he is the heir of an earlier Viking who ruled the country) but he gives it a try. He sails to England and sacks and burns a few towns.

Harald Hardrada reaches York, the largest town in northern England. His awesome army absolutely thrashes Edwin and Morcar and the city falls to the Norwegian king.

Duke William of Normandy

A descendant of Rollo the Viking who claims he is Edward's first and only choice.

William (a distant cousin of Edward) is one angry dude. He says that Edward promised him ages ago the crown was his. He gets a fleet ready to invade, but strong winds stop him from going anywhere.

In September, William is still stuck in Normandy, but his luck is about to change. King Harold's fleet are out of supplies, and while they restock, the southern coast of England is unprotected.

Round three

The Vikings say goodbye

Harald Hardrada's once-mighty army loses so many men at Stamford Bridge that only 24 of the original fleet of 240 longships are needed to take survivors back home to Norway. Up until now, the word "defeat" has not been in the Viking dictionary. Dude, it feels like the end of an era. Will the Vikings really sail off into the sunset?

Round four

On September 25, King Harold's army makes a surprise attack on the Viking camp near Stamford Bridge. The Vikings are caught completely off guard, but soon the battle is raging. Harald Hardrada is killed. It is a stunning defeat.

King Harold and his army head south to battle William's army near Hastings. William's Norman archers rain arrows on Harold's line of men. The battle lasts all day, but then an arrow strikes Harold right in the eye, and the king croaks.

William gets another lucky break. The wind changes at last, and he is able to set sail for England with the Norman fleet. He lands on the southern coast, and William and his warriors march to Hastings. It's all going down now, people.

King Harold's death creates a job opening—the throne of England. Both of William's rivals are pushing up daisies now. On December 25, 1066, he is crowned king of England. That's one dude who really gets what he wants for Christmas.

Timeline

So many places to raid, so many people to terrify…and so little time. For 300 years, the Vikings rock the world. They cross the oceans and continents in search of land, treasure, and trade opportunities. Their brave and daring explorers reach parts of the world that are completely unheard of back home in Sweden, Norway, and Denmark. Their skills at sea and superb shipbuilding dazzle everybody. The full-on and ferocious attacks they launch are the stuff of legends. As surely as they carve their names on runestones, they carve out a place in history, dude.

793
Vikings from Norway attack monastery of Lindisfarne, England.

798
Vikings launch attacks on towns and churches in France.

825
Norwegian Vikings led by Floki Raven reach Iceland. Cool.

795
Vikings sail to the Irish Sea, and begin raiding Ireland.

840
Viking settlers found the city of Dublin, Ireland.

1000
Leif Erikson explores the east coast of North America.

991
English king Ethelred pays the first Danegeld ransom payment.

1010
Viking explorer Throfinn Karlsefni founds a settlement in Vineland, North America.

1000
The Greenlanders and Icelanders convert to Christianity. Holy moly.

1013
The Danes take over England. English king Ethelred runs away.

1015
Vikings decide to abandon the settlement at Vineland.

1016
Danish ruler King Canute takes charge of England.

1042
Edward the Confessor becomes king of England.

1047
Harald Hardrada makes himself sole king of Norway.

1000 (Leif Erikson)

844

Vikings raid the town of Seville in Spain. Ole, dude!

860

Viking raids on the grand city of Constantinople.

865

An awesome army led by Ivar the Boneless invades England.

872

Hairy Harald the Shaggy becomes king of Norway.

878

England's King Alfred the Great defeats a Viking army.

857

Oh la la… Vikings attack Paris, France.

862

Viking settlers found a trading center at Novgorod, Russia.

900

Vikings raid up and down the Mediterranean coast.

981

Viking outlaw Eric the Red explores Greenland and sets up a colony.

930

The first Thing parliament takes place in Iceland. A cool thing.

960

Danish king Harald Bluetooth converts to Christianity.

911

French king grants land to Viking chief Rollo, where he establishes Normandy.

1066

King Harold of England gets an eyeful in battle.

1066

William of Normandy becomes king of England. The end.

KEY

Viking homelands

Places where Vikings settled

63

INDEX

ACKNOWLEDGMENTS

Rich Cando dedicates this book to the following dudes:

Friends, family, and fans for supporting the expansion of the "Dude" universe, and specifically Richard and JoAnn Cando for making my personal history possible.

Laura Buller dedicates this book to:
Alice (you rule) and Sean (you rock).

Dorling Kindersley would like to thank: Constance Novis for proofreading.

The illustrator would like to thank:
Assistant illustrators: Anthony Conley, Nicolette Davenport, Warren Lee, Zim McCurtis, James Morphew, Keith Tiernan, Steffen Vala

Assistant sketch artists: Erin Fusco, Mike Robinson, Misaki Sawada, Steffen Vala

Color corrections: Melissa Bolosan, Rodney Collins, James Morphew, Leslie Saiz

Rich Cando's representation: Hal Kant

The author would like to give big ups to all the young dudes at DK: Julie Ferris, Jim Green, Andrea Mills, Diane Thistlethwaite, and Lin Esposito, and props to Peter Chrisp for keeping it real.